HEALTH Need to Know

SilverTip

Smoking and Vaping

by Ashley Kuehl

Consultant: Caitlin Krieck, Social Studies Teacher and Instructional Coach, The Lab School of Washington

BEARPORT
PUBLISHING

Minneapolis, Minnesota

Credits

Cover and title page, © Elena Belodedova/Shutterstock; 3, © irin-k/Shutterstock; 4–5, © Sophon Nawit/Shutterstock; 7, © flaviano fabrizi/Shutterstock; 9, © Diego Cervo/Shutterstock; 11, © robin/Adobe Stock; 13, © Aleksandr Yu/Shutterstock; 15, © siro46/Shutterstock; 17, © Kateryna Onyshchuk/Shutterstock; 19, © Edward Roth/Alamy Stock Photo; 21, © MollyNZ/iStock; 23, © PA Images/Alamy Stock Photo; 25, © R Kawka/ Alamy Stock Photo; 27, © wundervisuals/iStock; 28, © somchaisom/iStock.

Bearport Publishing Company Product Development Team

Publisher: Jen Jenson; Director of Product Development: Spencer Brinker; Editorial Director: Allison Juda; Editor: Cole Nelson; Editor: Tiana Tran; Production Editor: Naomi Reich; Art Director: Kim Jones; Designer: Kayla Eggert; Designer: Steve Scheluchin; Production Specialist: Owen Hamlin

Statement on Usage of Generative Artificial Intelligence

Bearport Publishing remains committed to publishing high-quality nonfiction books. Therefore, we restrict the use of generative AI to ensure accuracy of all text and visual components pertaining to a book's subject. See BearportPublishing.com for details.

Library of Congress Cataloging-in-Publication Data is available at www.loc.gov or upon request from the publisher.

ISBN: 979-8-89577-076-4 (hardcover)
ISBN: 979-8-89577-523-3 (paperback)
ISBN: 979-8-89577-193-8 (ebook)

Copyright © 2026 Bearport Publishing Company. All rights reserved. No part of this publication may be reproduced in whole or in part, stored in any retrieval system, or transmitted in any form or by any means, electronic, mechanical, photocopying, recording, or otherwise, without written permission from the publisher. Bearport Publishing is a division of FlutterBee Education Group.

For more information, write to Bearport Publishing, 3500 American Blvd W, Suite 150, Bloomington, MN 55431.

Contents

Not So Nice 4
Tobacco. 6
The Body on Tobacco 8
E-Smoking 12
Can't Stop 16
It's All About the Youth 18
Those Are the Rules 22
Taking Care of You 26

What's in a Cigarette? 28
SilverTips for Success 29
Glossary 30
Read More 31
Learn More Online 31
Index 32
About the Author 32

Not So Nice

Your friend draws a breath from something that looks like a pen. A strange mist comes from the object. Your friend is using an e-cigarette, also known as **vaping**.

Lots of people vape. It may seem harmless, but vaping is dangerous.

E-cigarettes come in many different shapes, sizes, and colors. They also have different names. Some common ones include vapes, vape pens, and mods.

Tobacco

Vaping and smoking are similar. Both include breathing in gas through the mouth and into the lungs.

One big difference is that cigarettes have **tobacco**. The tobacco plant's leaves are dried and ground up. Then, they are rolled into a paper tube and smoked. Cigars are also made with tobacco.

Some kinds of tobacco are not smoked. One type is dry snuff. People breathe the leaves directly into their noses. Another is chewing tobacco. Users hold this tobacco in their mouths or chew it.

Tobacco plants

The Body on Tobacco

There are many bad **chemicals** in tobacco. One is **nicotine**. It is very **addictive**. When someone uses tobacco, nicotine goes into their blood. The brain makes **endorphins** (en-DOR-finz). The person's heartbeat and breathing get faster. At first, endorphins make the person feel good. But this feeling passes quickly.

> Over time, nicotine makes it harder for the brain to work. It can cause headaches and dizziness. Nicotine may make people feel tired, angry, or sad.

Tobacco smoke has at least 70 chemicals that cause cancer. Arsenic, tar, and carbon monoxide are just a few. Some chemicals in tobacco smoke can lead to heart and lung **diseases**. In the United States, smoking causes about 480,000 deaths a year.

> Even breathing in someone else's tobacco smoke is bad. Each year, this **secondhand** smoke causes about 41,000 deaths in the United States.

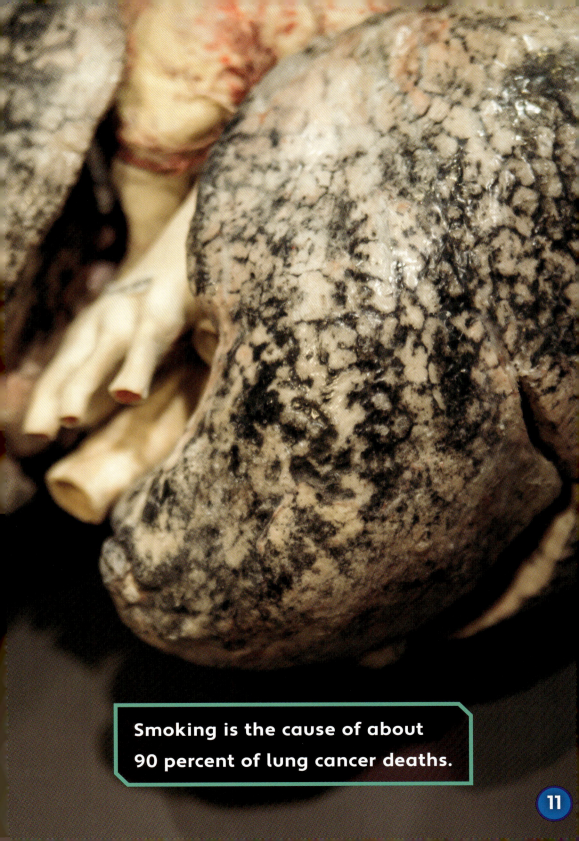

Smoking is the cause of about 90 percent of lung cancer deaths.

E-Smoking

E-cigarettes do not contain tobacco. Instead, most vapes are filled with a liquid made of nicotine and other chemicals. A battery-powered heating system warms up the liquid. This turns it into a mist. Users breathe in the mist through their mouths and into their lungs.

> Some e-cigarettes come with **cartridges**. They can be refilled. The cartridges used to come in many different flavors, such as grape and watermelon. This made many teens try vaping. In 2020, most flavors were banned.

Just because vapes don't have tobacco, doesn't mean they are safe. The nicotine in vapes is just as addictive as that found in cigarettes. It can cause nausea and diarrhea. Heavy metals and other chemicals in vaping mist can also cause cancer.

Vaping can lead to EVALI. This is short for e-cigarette or vaping use-associated lung injury. It is a lung disease that can cause chest pains and fevers.

Vaping can make people feel sick.

Can't Stop

Once people start smoking or vaping, it's hard to stop. They get an addiction to nicotine. People feel unwell if they stop using it. Sometimes, they feel angry or have headaches. Using nicotine again makes those feelings go away. Addiction makes it very hard to stop smoking or vaping.

> In 2024, almost 6 percent of middle and high school students in the United States used e-cigarettes. About 64 percent said they wanted to quit.

It's All About the Youth

Many smoking and vaping companies **advertise** to young people. They want teens to try their products and become addicted.

Young people with nicotine addictions often become lifelong smokers or vapers. They will buy many products. This gives a lot of money to the companies.

> In the 1930s, tobacco companies made ads telling people that doctors said cigarettes were healthy. Companies also used famous people in their ads.

In the 1950s, researchers proved that smoking was dangerous. Over time, fewer people started smoking cigarettes. Tobacco companies lost money. In the 2000s, they began selling vaping products as well. Companies said vaping could help people stop smoking. But vaping soon became popular with young non-smokers.

> Most people who start vaping have never smoked tobacco. Between 2011 and 2015, e-cigarette use rose 900 percent among high school students!

Those Are the Rules

Many laws were made to stop people from smoking. People must be at least 21 years old to buy tobacco. Tobacco companies are no longer allowed to advertise to children. There is also a **tax** on tobacco products. Since they cost more, people may be less likely to buy them.

> In 1999, the U.S. Department of Justice sued several tobacco companies. The government said these companies had lied about the effects of tobacco. In the end, they were found guilty.

One law says tobacco products must have warning labels.

At first, tobacco laws did not apply to vaping products. But laws are changing. Most states do not allow people to vape in workplaces or restaurants. In 2019, it became illegal for people under 21 to buy e-cigarettes in the United States. Some states also have taxes on vaping products.

> Some states have laws about the boxes and labels of vaping products. The boxes must say these products are for adults. They also must be hard for children to open.

Taking Care of You

Making smart choices is important for your body. This means avoiding unhealthy activities, such as smoking and vaping. It can be hard to say no. But no one else can make that choice for you.

You only get one body. It's your job to take care of it.

> Smoking and vaping is more dangerous for teens. That's because young brains are still growing. Smoking and vaping can cause damage with lasting harm.

What's in a Cigarette?

Cigarettes have many chemicals that can cause harm. The following are just a few of the dangerous chemicals in cigarettes.

Tar
This makes yellow stains on teeth and fingernails.

Nicotine
A chemical that raises blood pressure. It also makes the heart beat faster.

Carbon monoxide
This causes blood vessels to hold less oxygen.

Cyanide
This makes it hard for the body to take in and use oxygen.

Arsenic
A chemical that causes cancer and lung disease.

SilverTips for SUCCESS

★ SilverTips for REVIEW

Review what you've learned. Use the text to help you.

Define key terms

    addiction   tobacco
    nicotine   vaping
    smoking

Check for understanding

What do smoking and vaping do to the body?

Why do tobacco companies advertise to young people?

Why is it hard for people to stop smoking or vaping?

Think deeper

How may a person's life change if they start smoking or vaping?

★ SilverTips on TEST-TAKING

- **Make a study plan.** Ask your teacher what the test is going to cover. Then, set aside time to study a little bit every day.

- **Read all the questions carefully.** Be sure you know what is being asked.

- **Skip any questions** you don't know how to answer right away. Mark them and come back later if you have time.

Glossary

addictive causing a strong physical and mental need

advertise to present products for sale

cartridges small containers containing a liquid that can be swapped out and refilled

chemicals substances that have certain traits

diseases illnesses

endorphins brain chemicals that make people feel good

nicotine a substance found in smoking and vaping products that can cause addiction and other health problems

secondhand already used by or coming from someone else

tax money paid to a government so that it can provide services to people

tobacco a plant used to make cigarettes and other smoking products

vaping breathing in mist from an e-cigarette

Read More

Crawford, Bev. *What Are the Risks of Vaping? (Questions Explored).* San Diego, CA: BrightPoint Press, 2023.

Faust, D. R. *The Circulatory System (Body Systems: Need to Know).* Minneapolis: Bearport Publishing Company, 2025.

Holmes, Kirsty. *Healthy Body (Live Well!).* Minneapolis: Bearport Publishing Company, 2024.

Learn More Online

1. Go to **FactSurfer.com** or scan the QR code below.
2. Enter "**Smoking and Vaping**" into the search box.
3. Click on the cover of this book to see a list of websites.

Index

addiction 16, 18

advertising 18, 22

cancer 10, 14, 28

companies 18, 20, 22

e-cigarettes 4, 12, 14, 16, 20, 24

laws 22–24

liquids 12

nicotine 8, 12, 14, 16, 28

products 18, 20, 22–24

quitting 16

researchers 20

secondhand smoke 10

taxes 22, 24

teens 12, 18, 26

tobacco 6–8, 10, 12, 14, 18, 20, 22–24

About the Author

Ashley Kuehl is an editor and writer specializing in nonfiction for young people. She lives in Minneapolis, MN.